RUSSELL HYLTON

The Jesus Journey

A Roadmap For The Born-Again Life

First published by Russell Hylton 2026

Copyright © 2026 by Russell Hylton

All rights reserved. No part of this publication may be reproduced, stored or transmitted in any form or by any means, electronic, mechanical, photocopying, recording, scanning, or otherwise without written permission from the publisher. It is illegal to copy this book, post it to a website, or distribute it by any other means without permission.

For more information, visit www.russellhylton

First edition

ISBN: 9798245234731

This book was professionally typeset on Reedsy.
Find out more at reedsy.com

Therefore if any man be in Christ, he is a new creature: old things are passed away; behold, all things are become new.
(2 Corinthians 5:17 KJV)

Contents

Preface		iii
How to Use This 21 Day Devotional		iv
You Have Received Jesus		v
Introduction		1
1	WELCOME TO THE JOURNEY	3
2	WHAT'S THE NEXT STEP ON THE JOURNEY?	6
3	WHO DOES THE BIBLE SAY GOD IS?	9
4	HOW DOES GOD GUIDE ME IN EVERYDAY LIFE?	11
5	WATER BAPTISM	14
6	GETTING TO KNOW GOD	17
7	WHAT IS GOD SHOWING ME?	20
8	HOW IS JESUS FORMING ME?	23
9	WHAT'S THE BEST WAY TO READ THE BIBLE?	26
10	LEARNING HOW TO PRAY	29
11	HEALTHY FRIENDSHIPS	32
12	EMBRACING WORSHIP	34
13	UNHEALTHY HABITS	37
14	LEARN TO TAKE A BREAK	40
15	UNDERSTANDING THE WAY JESUS LOVED	43
16	MAKE OTHERS FEEL AT HOME	46
17	GIVING	49
18	HELPING OTHERS	52
19	FORGIVE & FORGIVE SOME MORE	55
20	SHARING MY FAITH WITH OTHERS	58
21	YOU'RE JUST GETTING STARTED	61
22	SO, WHAT NOW?	64

NEXT STEPS	66
NOTES	69
NOTES	70
NOTES	71
NOTES	72
QUICK OVERVIEW	73

Preface

Heaven is celebrating right now, and so are we, because you have made a life changing decision to begin a new life in Christ.

This 21 Day Devotional was created just for you. Over the next twenty one days, you will be guided step by step as you learn what it means to follow Jesus, grow in your faith, and build real spiritual habits that can shape the rest of your life. Each day is designed to help you pause, pray, reflect, and move forward with purpose.

We prepared this material with you in mind, believing it will strengthen you as you take your first steps walking with Jesus. As you read each day, do it prayerfully, inviting the Holy Spirit to speak to your heart and lead you in every decision along the way.

We are praying for you daily throughout these twenty one days, and we encourage you to connect with a Bible teaching church as soon as possible. There you will find community, encouragement, and people who will walk beside you as you grow.

You are loved, chosen, and never alone on this journey. This is just the beginning.

Every blessing,
Pastors Russell & Beverly Hylton
www.russellhylton.com

How to Use This 21 Day Devotional

Set aside a few minutes each day for the next twenty one days. Find a quiet space where you can focus and be honest with God. Each day includes a short reading, Scripture, and a moment to pray and reflect.

Read slowly. Don't rush. Let God speak to you through His Word and through what's happening in your heart. Some days will challenge you. Some days will encourage you. All of them are meant to help you grow.

Be real in your prayers. You don't need perfect words. Just talk to God the way you would talk to someone who truly cares about you...because He does.

If you miss a day, don't quit. Just pick back up where you left off. Growth is a journey, not a race.

Most importantly, be open. God is doing something new in you, and these next twenty one days are just the beginning.

You Have Received Jesus

Throughout your life, you have made many decisions about what you believe—whether it's about politics, faith, where to live, or who to marry. Some decisions are easy; others take time to gather information and think through carefully. The decision you have made today—to follow Jesus—has the power to bring healing, growth, and restoration into every part of your life.

Let me ask you a very important question: If you were to leave this earth today, where would you spend eternity?

The Bible tells us clearly:

- *For this is how God loved the world: He gave his one and only Son, so that everyone who believes in him will not perish but have eternal life.* (**John 3:16 NLT**)

God loves you deeply, and He has a wonderful plan for your life. He wants every person to receive His free gift of salvation and everlasting life.

Let me ask you another question: If you believed something that wasn't true, would you want to know the truth?

Many people believe that being a good person is enough to get to heaven. But the Bible says:

- *For everyone has sinned; we all fall short of God's glorious standard.* (**Romans 3:23 NLT**)

- *For the wages of sin is death, but the free gift of God is eternal life through Christ Jesus our Lord.* (**Romans 6:23 NLT**)

God knows we want to live upright lives and do what is right. He also knows that as humans we are weak and cannot overcome sin on our own. That is why He sent His Son, Jesus, to take our place and die for our sins. There is power in the shed blood of Jesus. When we come to God and ask for forgiveness, the blood of Jesus covers our sins completely. We are no longer guilty.

Salvation Is a Free Gift

Receiving salvation is simple. All you need to do is invite Jesus Christ into your life as your Lord and Savior.

- *God saved you by his grace when you believed. And you can't take credit for this; it is a gift from God. Salvation is not a reward for the good things we have done, so none of us can boast about it.* (**Ephesians 2:8-9 NLT**)

The Bible explains exactly how to receive this gift:

- *If you openly declare that Jesus is Lord and believe in your heart that God raised him from the dead,* **you will be saved**. *For it is by believing in your heart that you are made right with God, and it is by openly declaring your faith that you are saved.* (**Romans 10:9-10 NLT**)

In other words, pray from your heart a simple, honest prayer like this:

Lord Jesus,

I ask You to come into my life and be my Lord and Savior. I believe You died for my sins and rose victorious over death. Forgive me for all my sins. I turn from sin today and choose to follow You all the days of my life. Lord, I give You all my pain, all my hurts, all my fears, and all my weaknesses. Today I receive complete healing in every area of my life. Because of Your shed blood, from this day forward I am a new creation in Christ Jesus. Thank You, Lord!

Introduction

You have made a powerful decision to follow Jesus, and I want you to know how significant that moment truly is. Saying yes to Him is not the end of something...it is the beginning of a brand new life. What you have stepped into is a journey that unfolds one day at a time, with grace leading the way.

This guide was created to help you take those first steps with confidence and clarity. Inside these pages, you will find Scripture, reflection, and simple practices designed to help you understand what your faith means and how it begins to shape your everyday life. This is a space for growth, discovery, and honest learning.

As you move forward, questions will naturally arise. How does this change my life? What should I do next? How do I grow in my walk with Jesus? You do not need to have every answer right now. Spiritual growth is not rushed...it is formed through consistency, obedience, and time with God.

This material is organized into 21 days, but I encourage you to move at a pace that best supports your growth. Whether it takes weeks, months, or becomes something you return to often, the goal is not simply to finish the pages. The goal is direction, confidence, and learning how to live out your faith in practical ways.

Following Jesus is a lifelong journey built on daily decisions to move forward with Him. I am honored to walk with you in this season, and I look forward to seeing all that God will continue to do in and through your life.

With gratitude and faith,
Bishop Russell Hylton

1

WELCOME TO THE JOURNEY

You said yes to Jesus and that is a big deal. Bigger than you might feel right now. Bigger than a moment. Bigger than a prayer. It is the start of something brand new.

People describe this decision in different ways. You might hear phrases like giving your life to Jesus, becoming a Christian, getting saved, or choosing to follow Him. The words may sound different, but they all point to the same reality.

You responded to God's invitation. So now the real questions start showing up.

- What actually changes because of this?
- What stays the same?
- And what does following Jesus really look like in everyday life?

That is what this journey is here to help you discover. Saying yes to Jesus means choosing to follow Him. Following Him means learning to live the way He lived. But before we talk about that, it helps to understand who Jesus is and why His life matters so much to yours.

The story starts at the very beginning. The Bible tells us that God created the world and created people on purpose. We were made to enjoy life, take care of what God created, and live connected to Him. But people made choices that caused damage to ourselves, to others, and to the world around us. The Bible calls that sin. Sin broke the relationship between a perfect God and imperfect people, making it impossible for us to fix things on our own.

But God did not walk away. Instead, He stepped in. God sent His son, Jesus, into the world. Jesus lived among people, experienced real life, and showed us what love, truth, and obedience actually look like. After about thirty three years, Jesus did what no one else could do. He took the weight of sin on Himself by dying on a cross, then defeated death by rising again and restoring our relationship with God.

Why would He do that? One night, Jesus talked with a man named Nicodemus who had honest questions about faith and life. In that conversation, Jesus said something that explains everything.

- **John 3:16–17 NLT** *"For this is how God loved the world. He gave his one and only Son, so that everyone who believes in him will not perish but have eternal life. God sent his Son into the world not to judge the world, but to save the world through him."*

That is the heart of it. God loves you so much that Jesus was willing to give His life so you could be forgiven, restored, and brought into God's family. Saying yes to Jesus means saying yes to that love, that grace, and that new way of living.

Tomorrow, we will talk more about how this new life begins to take shape. For today, take a moment to talk to God. You do not need fancy words. Just honesty.

Prayer

"God, I choose to trust Jesus today. I believe He is Your Son and that He came to save me and the world. I do not have everything figured out yet, but I want to follow Him and learn His way of living. Thank You for loving me. Thank You for welcoming me into Your family. Amen."

2

WHAT'S THE NEXT STEP ON THE JOURNEY?

Yesterday we ended with prayer, and today we will start with it, because God welcomes hearing from us at any time.

Prayer
"God, thank You for the gift of salvation saving me from myself and drawing me into a healing relationship with You. Let Your love shape me today, this week, and for the rest of my life. I'm trusting You to make me new. In Jesus' name, amen."

We end prayers "in Jesus' name" because that is how Jesus instructed us to pray. Thanks to what He did on the cross, we can talk to God directly, as family. That close connection is what empowers us to live like Him and grow into who He calls us to be.

Jesus lived with integrity. He loved those others rejected, spoke against injustice, and welcomed the outcasts. When we say yes to Jesus, we begin a lifelong process of following Him, and over time, His character begins to form in us. Jesus summed up the Bible's commandments this way: *love God with all that you are, and love your neighbor as yourself.*

But does this happen automatically, or do we play a part? It is both. God does the primary work, but we partner with Him.

- *He himself is the sacrifice that atones for our sins—and not only our sins but the sins of all the world.* (**1 John 2:2 NLT**)
- *But those who obey God's word truly show how completely they love him. That is how we know we are living in him. Those who say they live in God should live their lives as Jesus did.* (**1 John 2:5-6 NLT**)

Becoming more like Jesus is a process. God does the heavy lifting, but we partner with Him each day.

For the rest of this journey, we will focus on three ways to partner with Him:

1. Learning the basics of following Jesus Who is God? What does talking to Him look like? What are some good next steps? This week we will address questions like these.

2. Living like Jesus lived Jesus modeled ways of living that draw us closer to God. These are called spiritual practices, such as prayer, worship, and serving. In week two, we will explore some of these practices.

3. Loving like Jesus loved Nothing helps us grow more like Jesus than loving others as He did. In week three, we will look at what it means to put His love into practice.

Pause and reflect (journal it or discuss it with a friend):

- What parts of my life do I hope God will make new?
- How do I want to partner with Him to care for others and the world around me?

Let us continue. Jesus is with you. What is one thing you hope to see Him change in you? Pray about it now.

3

WHO DOES THE BIBLE SAY GOD IS?

Is God the Father? Is God Jesus the Son? Is God the Holy Spirit? Or is God all three in one?
Yes—all three in one.

When you choose to follow Jesus, you are making a three-in-one decision. You are accepting the invitation through Jesus (the Son of God) to become a child of God the Father, filled with the Holy Spirit, and empowered to live as a son or daughter of God. God exists as one being in three persons—the Trinity.

We see this beautiful picture of the Trinity throughout the Bible. Right from the beginning of Creation, the Spirit of God is present alongside God the Father. The first two verses of the Bible show this clearly:

- *In the beginning God created the heavens and the earth. The earth was formless and empty, and darkness covered the deep waters. And the Spirit of God was hovering over the surface of the waters.* (**Genesis 1:1-2 NLT**)

Later, the Gospel of John retells the story of Creation and includes Jesus. The author calls Him the Word, and describes Him as God. Reading the entire book of John is a great next step. Here are key verses from John 1 that reveal the three persons of God:

- *In the beginning the Word already existed. The Word was with God, and the Word was God. He existed in the beginning with God.* (**John 1:1-2 NLT**)

- *But to all who believed him and accepted him, he gave the right to become children of God.* (**John 1:12 NLT**)

- *So the Word became human and made his home among us. He was full of unfailing love and faithfulness. And we have seen his glory, the glory of the Father's one and only Son.* (**John 1:14 NLT**)

- *No one has ever seen God. But the unique One, who is himself God, is near to the Father's heart. He has revealed God to us.* (**John 1:18 NLT**)

- *Then John testified, "I saw the Holy Spirit descending like a dove from heaven and resting upon him. I didn't know he was the one, but when God sent me to baptize with water, he told me, 'The one on whom you see the Spirit descend and rest is the one who will baptize with the Holy Spirit.' I saw this happen to Jesus, so I testify that he is the Chosen One of God."* (**John 1:32-34 NLT**)

Here is the main point: Jesus, God the Father, and the Holy Spirit are one God. Jesus came not only to show us what God is like, but to give us direct access to the Father forever through the Holy Spirit.

Prayer

"God, help me to know You as Father, Son, and Holy Spirit. Father, You are my Provider. Jesus, You are my Savior. Holy Spirit, You are my Guide. In Jesus' name, amen."

4

HOW DOES GOD GUIDE ME IN EVERYDAY LIFE?

Yesterday we prayed: God, help me to know You as Father, Son, and Holy Spirit. Holy Spirit, You are my Guide.

Who is the Holy Spirit, and how does He guide us? Do we need to act especially spiritual to earn His attention? Jesus promised something far different.

Jesus described the Holy Spirit as a comforter, advocate, helper, and friend. Think of someone in your life who fits that description—a mentor, a caring parent, or a trusted friend. As you read Jesus' words, picture the Holy Spirit in those same roles for you: Comforter, Advocate, Helper, and Friend.

- *And I will ask the Father, and he will give you another Advocate, who will never leave you. He is the Holy Spirit, who leads into all truth. The world cannot receive him, because it isn't looking for him and doesn't recognize him. But you know him, because he lives with you now and later will be in you.* (**John 14:16-17 NLT**)

Jesus spoke these words to His followers as He prepared them for His departure to be with the Father. They may have felt uncertain, anxious, or even abandoned, but Jesus reassured them.

- *But in fact, it is best for you that I go away, because if I don't, the Advocate won't come. If I do go away, then I will send him to you.* (**John 16:7 NLT**)

His leaving was not about distance; it was about drawing even closer. The Holy Spirit would not only be with them—He would live within them.

- *No, I will not abandon you as orphans—I will come to you. Soon the world will no longer see me, but you will see me. Since I live, you also will live. When I am raised to life again, you will know that I am in my Father, and you are in me, and I am in you.* (**John 14:18-20 NLT**)

Jesus was coming closer through the Holy Spirit, who would fill His followers with the same comfort, power, and love that filled Jesus Himself.

When we say yes to following Jesus' way, we invite the Holy Spirit to help, comfort, and advocate for us—and through us.

- *But when the Father sends the Advocate as my representative—that is, the Holy Spirit—he will teach you everything and will remind you of everything I have told you.* (**John 14:26 NLT**)

God chooses to live within us and guide us from the inside. In the weeks ahead, we will explore practices that help us become more open and welcoming to

God's presence in our daily lives.

Prayer

"God, thank You for the Holy Spirit. Please continue to help me know You as Comforter, Helper, Advocate, and Friend. I trust You to guide me as I follow the way of Jesus. In Jesus' name, amen."

5

WATER BAPTISM

In the past few days, we have explored God's three-in-one nature as Father, Son, and Holy Spirit, and how God lives in us today through the Holy Spirit. Today, we will look at another Bible story that includes all three persons of the Trinity. The main focus is baptism.

Baptism is a public way that followers of Jesus declare their decision to follow Him. A pastor or trusted friend stands with you in a pool or another body of water. They help you lean back into the water and then bring you right back up.

Why go underwater? Baptism is a powerful symbol of Jesus' death, resurrection, and the new life we receive through Him.

Going under the water represents your old life and sins being washed away through Jesus' death on the cross. Coming up out of the water pictures being raised to new life, just as Jesus was raised from the dead.

This public step mirrors the way Jesus Himself was baptized.

- *Then Jesus went from Galilee to the Jordan River to be baptized by John. But John tried to talk him out of it. "I am the one who needs to be baptized by you," he said, "so why are you coming to me?" But Jesus said, "It should be done, for we must carry out all that God requires." So John agreed to baptize him. After his baptism, as Jesus came up out of the water, the heavens were opened and he saw the Spirit of God descending like a dove and settling on him. And a voice from heaven said, "This is my dearly loved Son, who brings me great joy."* (**Matthew 3:13-17 NLT**)

Now, reread the story and place yourself in the scene as the one being baptized by John. Imagine the feel of the water. What is it like to hear God's voice of approval? What does God say to you personally? How do you sense the Holy Spirit's presence?

Near the end of His time on earth, Jesus gathered His followers and gave them this mission:

- *Therefore, go and make disciples of all the nations, baptizing them in the name of the Father and the Son and the Holy Spirit.* (**Matthew 28:19 NLT**)

When you have said yes to Jesus and chosen to follow His way of life, baptism is one of the next steps you are invited to take. It is a clear, public declaration to everyone: "I have decided to follow Jesus."

Pause and reflect (journal it or talk it over with a friend):

- Have you been baptized?
- What would it feel like for you to take this step of following Jesus?
- What questions do you still have about baptism?

Prayer

"God, thank You for the example of Jesus' baptism and for inviting me into this step of faith. Help me understand what baptism means and show me if it is the next step for me. Fill me with Your Spirit as I follow You. In Jesus' name, amen."

6

GETTING TO KNOW GOD

How do you get to know someone new? Most of us build a friendship by asking questions, spending time together, and sharing meaningful stories from our lives.

Getting to know God can feel a little different from grabbing tacos with friends, but the same basic principles apply: time, conversation, and openness. So how do we grow in knowing God?

Here are three key ways to start and build that relationship.

1. **We spend time with God through prayer.** Prayer is simply communicating with God. You can thank Him for who He is, share your excitement or needs, ask for help, or even sit quietly in His presence. Prayer is not a performance, so there is no need to worry about saying the "right" words. Be honest. If something matters to you, bring it to God. He loves you and listens. Since God's Spirit lives in you, pay attention to ways He might speak to your heart as you pray or go through your day.

2. **We read the Bible.** The Bible is a collection of books written thousands of years ago by people inspired by God. Why read it today? The Bible shows us what God is like and how people have come to know Him.

Guided by the Holy Spirit, its authors share stories of God's goodness, ask honest questions, and face the hardest parts of life. Through these pages, we see God's character—His kindness, forgiveness, justice, and love—especially lived out in the life of Jesus. Reading the Bible helps us understand God more deeply and see how He relates to us.

3. **We gather with other followers of Jesus.** Knowing God is both personal ("Jesus and me") and shared ("Jesus and we"). The Bible encourages us to stay connected with others who follow Him.

- *Let us think of ways to motivate one another to acts of love and good works. And let us not neglect our meeting together, as some people do, but encourage one another, especially now that the day of his return is drawing near.* (**Hebrews 10:24-25 NLT**)

When we meet together, we hear stories of God's faithfulness, listen to wisdom from Scripture, sing songs about His love, and encourage one another. A simple and powerful way to build this habit is to regularly attend church. It gives you the chance to make friends, share what God is doing in your life, and practice serving and encouraging others.

If you have not already, consider making a plan to join others at church this week. You might even invite a friend, family member, or neighbor to come along and experience the life-changing way of Jesus together.

Pause and reflect (journal it or talk it over with a friend):

- Which of these three ways feels most natural for you to start with right now?
- What is one small step you can take this week to get to know God more?

- Who could you invite to join you in gathering with other followers of Jesus?

Prayer

"God, thank You for wanting to be known by me. Help me grow closer to You through prayer, reading Your Word, and being with other believers. Open my heart to hear You and follow You more each day. In Jesus' name, amen."

7

WHAT IS GOD SHOWING ME?

Congratulations! You have made it to the end of week one.

We are truly glad you have taken these steps to grow in your faith. Choosing to follow Jesus is an important decision. It often brings new thoughts, questions, or even some uncertainty. That is normal and okay. Following Jesus is a lifelong journey, and we do not need to understand everything after just one week.

With that in mind, how are you feeling right now? Take a quiet moment to reflect.

Below is space to write two or three words or short phrases that describe your feelings about your faith journey so far. You might feel encouraged and hopeful, a bit uncertain, peaceful, or something else. There is no right or wrong way to answer. Your honest thoughts are what matter most here.

This is private—just for you and God. No one else needs to see it.

1.

2.

3.

This week we have seen that God loves us deeply, forgives us fully, and gives us purpose: to become more like Jesus day by day. We have also learned that He desires a close relationship with us and has given us meaningful ways to connect with Him.

We have only begun to explore what it means to follow Jesus. There is much more ahead, and we are thankful to continue this journey together.

As we finish week one and prepare for week two, think about one or two questions you have about God, faith, or the Bible. Write them down. Then, sometime this week, share them with a pastor, trusted friend, or mentor. Asking questions is a healthy part of growing.

Before you pray, read this verse slowly and let it settle in your heart:

- *And I am certain that God, who began the good work within you, will continue his work until it is finally finished on the day when Christ Jesus returns.* (**Philippians 1:6 NLT**)

This promise is for you. God started a good work in you, and He will faithfully continue it until it is complete.

Now speak to Him about what you wrote—your feelings, your questions, your hopes. Be open and honest. He is listening.

Prayer
"God, thank You for beginning this good work in me. Thank You for Your

patience with my questions and my journey. Help me trust that You will keep working in my life. Guide me as I continue to follow Jesus. In His name, amen."

You are doing meaningful work. Week two is ahead—let us keep going together.

8

HOW IS JESUS FORMING ME?

Welcome to week two of our journey! Last week we discovered that following Jesus starts with a real choice: accepting God's gift of forgiveness. That choice opens the door to a lifelong process of becoming more like Him.

You may be wondering: What does becoming more like Jesus actually look like in real life? Is it even possible?

Jesus is God—the Creator of everything, who has always existed and never sinned. How could we ever become like Him?

Think about it this way: How does someone become a concert violinist, a professional athlete, or an expert chef? They start somewhere. They say yes to a new way of living and learning. Saying yes doesn't make them an expert overnight, but it does make them a learner—one who is growing into something greater.

As learners, they gain knowledge, build relationships, practice skills, face setbacks, make mistakes, and keep pressing forward. The word Jesus used for this kind of learner is "disciple."

When we said yes to Jesus, we said yes to becoming His disciples for the long haul.

Over the next two weeks, we will explore what it means to live as a disciple of Jesus. First, we will look at some of the habits and mindsets Jesus valued and lived out—often called spiritual practices. Then, we will see how Jesus loved others and how we can show that same kind of sacrificial care in our own lives.

During Jesus' time on earth, some people asked Him what the greatest commandment was. Here is how He answered:

- *Jesus replied, "'You must love the Lord your God with all your heart, all your soul, and all your mind.' This is the first and greatest commandment. A second is equally important: 'Love your neighbor as yourself.' The entire law and all the demands of the prophets are based on these two commandments."* **(Matthew 22:37-40 NLT)**

Jesus boiled it all down to this: Love God with everything you are, and love your neighbor as yourself. Becoming the kind of person who truly lives that out is a lifelong journey.

Every disciple faces setbacks and failures. If you are like most of us, you may have already experienced some this week—falling back into an old habit, saying something you regret, or simply not living up to what you hoped. When that happens, we do not need to hide from God or others. His forgiving kindness is always there to pick us up and help us keep becoming more like Jesus.

Pause and reflect (journal it or talk it over with a friend):

- What is one area where you want to grow in love—for God, for yourself, or for others?

- What might it look like for you to take one small step forward this week?

Prayer

"God, You see every mistake I make. Thank You for Your forgiveness and for guiding me as I become more like Jesus. Holy Spirit, please help me see one step I can take today to grow in love for You, myself, and the people around me. In Jesus' name, amen."

9

WHAT'S THE BEST WAY TO READ THE BIBLE?

To Jesus, the Bible was much more than words on a page. God designed it to guide His followers through every generation in how to live and love in ways that reflect His heart. But how do we approach it? The Bible is a vast collection of ancient poetry, songs, history, laws, letters, and more.

Modern Bibles divide into two main sections: the Old Testament (also known as the Hebrew Bible) and the New Testament. The New Testament was written after Jesus lived on earth. Even though Jesus read only from the Old Testament during His time, the way He used Scripture can help us read the entire Bible today.

Let us look at two important ways Jesus engaged with the Bible.

First, Jesus used the Bible to reveal God's love for people. In Matthew 22, someone asked Jesus what the greatest commandment in the law was. We looked at this passage yesterday, but let us reread it and consider how it shapes our approach to Scripture.

- *Jesus replied, "You must love the Lord your God with all your heart, all your soul, and all your mind. This is the first and greatest commandment. A second is equally important: Love your neighbor as yourself. The entire law and all the demands of the prophets are based on these two commandments."* (**Matthew 22:37-40 NLT**)

Jesus quoted Scripture to help people understand God's heart and how He calls us to live. As we read the Bible, one helpful question to ask is: How do these words help me love God more deeply and love others more fully?

Second, Jesus used the Bible in its proper context. In Matthew 4, when Jesus faced temptation in the wilderness, the enemy quoted Scripture to twist the truth and make lies sound wise. Jesus was not misled because He understood the full context of God's Word.

The Bible was written in ancient languages, cultures, and situations very different from ours. When we read it, it helps to ask questions such as: Who wrote this? Who was it written to? What kind of writing is this, poetry, history, a letter, prophecy? What is happening in this book or chapter?

Reading without context can cause us to miss the intended meaning. In the worst cases, it might lead us to conclusions that go against God's way of life. When in doubt, return to this guiding question: How do these words help me love God and love my neighbor?

The Bible is more than words on a page. It is a gift from God with the power to change us from the inside out.

This is why it can be helpful to think of this practice as studying or learning the Bible, rather than just reading it. The Bible is meant to be read, reread, explored, meditated on, and reflected upon again and again.

Pause and reflect (journal it or talk it over with a friend):

- What is one question you can ask yourself the next time you open the Bible?
- How might focusing on loving God and others change the way you approach Scripture?

Prayer

"God, thank You for giving us Your Word. Help me read the Bible with an open heart. Teach me to see Your love in every page and to understand it in its true context. Guide me to grow in love for You and for others as I learn from Scripture. In Jesus' name, amen."

10

LEARNING HOW TO PRAY

Jesus spent a great deal of time in prayer. The Bible records several moments when He stayed up all night praying. Why would He do that? After all, He is God. Why did He need to pray?

While Jesus was fully God, He was also fully human during His time on earth. As a human, He experienced the same needs we do and relied on consistent habits to maintain His close relationship with God the Father. For Jesus, prayer was a source of guidance, courage, strength, and deep connection with God. The same can be true for us.

Consider one example: when Jesus was about to make a major decision—choosing the twelve disciples who would become the foundation of the church. Here is what the Bible says:

- *One of those days Jesus went out to a mountainside to pray, and spent the night praying to God. When morning came, he called his disciples to him and chose twelve of them, whom he also designated apostles.* (**Luke 6:12-13 NLT**)

Jesus did not pray only before big decisions. He also prayed to experience closeness with God and to find strength before facing challenging moments.

So how can we build a habit of prayer like Jesus did? First, let us consider how Jesus **did not** pray.

- Jesus did not use fancy or impressive words in His prayers.
- Jesus did not pray to put on a show for those around Him.
- Jesus did not come to God with a list of demands or expectations.

Prayer is meant to be a personal, honest conversation with God, much like you would talk with a close friend, family member, or trusted mentor. There is no pressure to get it "right." Release any idea of how you think prayer should sound and simply speak openly with God.

Now, let us look at how Jesus **did** pray. Jesus made prayer a priority in His life. Jesus prayed both in the presence of others and when He was alone. Jesus asked others to pray for Him.

Today, let us begin (or continue) a simple habit of prayer. Set aside just a few minutes—perhaps on your drive home, before bed, or first thing in the morning—to talk with God. Share what you are thankful for. Bring Him your needs and concerns. Ask for guidance. And take time to listen for His voice.

As you do this regularly, you will likely notice your relationship with Jesus growing closer and more real every day.

Pause and reflect (journal it or talk it over with a friend):

- What is one small moment in your day when you could pause to pray?
- What might you want to say to God first—thanks, a need, a question, or simply being present with Him?

Prayer

"God, thank You for inviting me into conversation with You. Help me make prayer a real part of my day. Teach me to speak honestly and to listen for Your voice. Draw me closer to Jesus through these moments. In His name, amen."

11

HEALTHY FRIENDSHIPS

Throughout His ministry, Jesus surrounded Himself with people who encouraged Him, prayed for Him, and stood with Him. Yes, Jesus was their Savior, but He was also their friend.

Here is how Jesus described His relationship with His followers:

- *I no longer call you servants, because a servant does not know his master's business. Instead, I have called you friends, for everything that I learned from my Father I have made known to you.* (**John 15:15 NLT**)

If Jesus intentionally chose close relationships, it is a good idea for us to do the same with other followers of Jesus.

Life can feel overwhelmingly hard at times, and in those moments we need people we can turn to for prayer, wisdom, and support. In times of joy, sharing those moments with friends makes them even richer and more meaningful.

This is true about relationships because God created us in His image. God exists in perfect, life-giving relationship as Father, Son, and Holy Spirit, and He desires relationship with us. That is why surrounding yourself with people who follow Jesus is an essential part of spiritual life. When you do, you are living out God's own example.

Do you have the close relationships you need right now? People who encourage your walk with Jesus and stand with you through life's ups and downs? If not, consider how you might invest more in the relationships you already have or begin seeking the friendships you are missing.

If you do not yet have close friends who follow Jesus, joining a small group of fellow believers is one of the best places to start.

Finding and building friendships can feel a little awkward or even intimidating at first, but finding your people is worth the effort. It is life-giving to have friends who celebrate you, support you, and encourage you to keep growing closer to Jesus every day.

Pause and reflect (journal it or talk it over with a friend):

- Who in your life encourages you in your faith right now?
- What is one small step you could take this week to connect more deeply with other followers of Jesus?

Prayer
"God, thank You for calling me Your friend through Jesus. Help me build meaningful relationships with other believers who point me to You. Give me courage to reach out, openness to invest in others, and wisdom to find the friendships I need. In Jesus' name, amen."

12

EMBRACING WORSHIP

When you gather with other followers of Jesus, learn Scripture together, pray to God, and build real, life-changing relationships, something beautiful happens: **worship.**

Jesus' life was full of worship. When you think of worship, what comes to mind? Words like music, instruments, or songs probably show up first—and that makes sense. Singing is definitely one way Jesus worshiped.

On the night before His death, Jesus shared a final meal with His closest friends. It was Passover, a deeply meaningful celebration for the Jewish people. At the close of the meal, Jesus and the disciples sang together. In that ancient tradition, people often sang Psalms 113 through 118 during Passover. It's very likely that Jesus joined in those songs of praise. Here are just a couple of the lines they may have sung:

- *Who is like the Lord our God, who is seated on high, who looks far down on the heavens and the earth? He raises the poor from the dust and lifts the needy from the ash heap, to make them sit with princes, with the princes of his people.* (**Psalm 113:5-8 NLT**)

- *Then I called on the name of the Lord: "O Lord, I pray, deliver my soul!" Gracious is the Lord, and righteous; our God is merciful. The Lord preserves the simple; when I was brought low, he saved me. Return, O my soul, to your rest; for the Lord has dealt bountifully with you.* (**Psalm 116:4-7 NLT**)

These words overflow with awe and celebrate who God is—His greatness as Creator and Ruler, His love that chooses to care for us even though He doesn't have to, and His special attention to those who are hurting physically or spiritually.

Today, just like that Passover gathering, worship services create space for people to come together and honor God. Worship songs give us the chance to remember who God is, what He has done, and to give Him the praise He deserves.

Singing is one powerful way to worship, but worship is much bigger than music alone.

We worship whenever we express our devotion and love to God. Worship happens when we recognize His incredible qualities and the amazing things He has done. A breathtaking sunset, the birth of a child, an answered prayer, or even a quiet moment of gratitude can all become acts of worship. Any time something reminds us of God's character and goodness, it becomes an opportunity to praise Him.

This weekend, you will have the chance to worship God through singing alongside other followers of Jesus at church. But don't wait until Sunday to worship.

Right now, take a few minutes. Think about what you are thankful for...maybe the beauty of creation, a meaningful relationship, God's forgiveness through Jesus, or simply His presence in your life. Speak your gratitude to Him. Tell

Him who He is to you and what He has done.

Pause and reflect (journal it or talk it over with a friend):

- What is one thing you are thankful for today that points to God's goodness
- How might you express that gratitude as worship, even in a small way?

Prayer

"God, thank You for who You are and for all You have done. Help me see moments of worship in everyday life. Open my heart to praise You through song, gratitude, and devotion. Draw me closer to You as I learn to worship in spirit and truth. In Jesus' name, amen."

13

UNHEALTHY HABITS

Do you ever find yourself wanting to do something even though you know it's wrong?

For three years, everything about Jesus' life felt uncomfortable. He spoke hard truths to people in power, faced constant criticism and attacks, and lived with the knowledge that people were plotting to kill Him. Yet early in His ministry, He was offered a way to skip all the suffering and take an easier path.

For forty days, Jesus was alone in the desert without food. In that moment of vulnerability, the devil offered Him shortcuts to avoid pain and gain power quickly. Temptation often comes when we are offered an easier route to something we want. Feeling tempted is not a sin. Giving in to it, however, can compromise who we are and pull us into cycles of regret and poor choices. The good news is we do not have to face temptation alone. We can look to Jesus.

Jesus overcame temptation through the spiritual practices He lived out every day. He knew the Scriptures deeply, and He knew His purpose. He understood that living out His calling would mean making hard, uncomfortable choices for the good of others. There was no easy way out, no shortcuts. Only by staying true to who He was and whose He was could He truly change the world.

Jesus refused to trade His identity and mission for temporary relief or pleasure.

We face temptations every day, both large and small, that try to pull us away from who God is shaping us to become. The encouraging truth is this: God wants to help you overcome them.

Here is what one follower of Jesus wrote about temptation:

- *No temptation has overtaken you except what is common to mankind. And God is faithful; he will not let you be tempted beyond what you can bear. But when you are tempted, he will also provide a way out so that you can endure it.* **(1 Corinthians 10:13 NLT)**

We can prepare for temptation before it comes, just as Jesus did. We do this by studying and believing God's Word, living out its truths, asking God for strength through prayer, sharing openly with trusted people, and watching for the escape routes God provides.

Sometimes the way out God offers looks practical: joining a recovery group, talking with a doctor or counselor, or meeting with a pastor to get the tools and support you need to walk in freedom.

You do not have to stay stuck. God is faithful, and He is already making a way for you.

Pause and reflect (journal it or talk it over with a friend):

- What is one temptation you are facing right now?
- What small step could you take this week to prepare or seek help when it comes?

Prayer

"Dear God, thank You for always giving me another chance. Help me recognize temptation when it comes and give me strength to resist it. Show me the way out You have prepared, and help me stay true to who You are calling me to be. In Jesus' name, amen."

14

LEARN TO TAKE A BREAK

Do you ever feel anxious about everything piling up during the week? Or wish you had more time for the people who matter most to you? If so, you are not alone. Life often feels like it demands constant busyness. But Jesus invites us to a different way, a better way.

Here is a surprising moment from Jesus' life:

- *Yet the news about him spread all the more, so that crowds of people came to hear him and to be healed of their sicknesses. But Jesus often withdrew to lonely places and prayed.* (**Luke 5:15-16 NLT**)

Think about what this says. Crowds were coming to hear Jesus teach and to receive healing, yet He chose to walk away. He stepped back from the demands so He could rest and pray. When Jesus chose rest over more productivity and more opportunities to help others, it was a good and necessary thing. Why?

We can only be as helpful to others as we are healthy ourselves. Like Jesus, we can set healthy boundaries with our time and intentionally slow down. Every human needs rest, and since Jesus was fully God and fully human while on earth, that need applied to Him too.

Rest is also an act of worship. The Bible opens with the story of God creating the world, structured over seven days. On the sixth day God created people, but the seventh day was set apart for rest.

Why does that matter? Because humanity's very first full day on earth was a day of rest, not work.

Throughout Scripture, the seventh day is called the Sabbath. On that day, people were invited to worship by stepping away from work. But how is rest itself worship?

It is easy to forget a basic spiritual truth: God is in control, and we are not. When we forget, we often try to control everything through constant work. We obsess over to-do lists, worry about falling behind, and push ourselves to the limit.

When we choose to pause, to set aside tasks and unfinished things, we are declaring that late projects, unfolded laundry, unread emails, or unmet expectations do not threaten God's plan for the world. That act of trust is worship.

You may work long hours or have people who depend on you. Do not feel guilty if a full day off each week is not possible right now. Instead, look for moments of rest when you can find them. Jesus did the same. Once, when He was weary, He simply sat down by a well. Another time, He napped in a boat during a storm.

So what about you? How might you build rest into your week? How can you weave small moments of rest into each day?

Pause and reflect (journal it or talk it over with a friend):

- What keeps you from resting right now?

- What is one small way you could intentionally slow down this week to trust God more?

Prayer

"God, thank You for the gift of rest and for showing us through Jesus that it is good and necessary. Help me trust You enough to pause, to step away from busyness, and to let go of what I cannot control. Teach me to rest in Your presence and to worship You by trusting Your plan. In Jesus' name, amen."

15

UNDERSTANDING THE WAY JESUS LOVED

Welcome to the final week of our journey! Last week we began exploring some spiritual practices that helped us live the way Jesus lived. We saw how His mindsets, habits, and daily choices created space for His ministry. This week we turn to the heart of it all: how Jesus loved. How did He relate to people? How did He make them feel? How did His words and actions fulfill His purpose?

Let us look at one moment when Jesus stepped in to correct an argument among His closest followers:

- *An argument started among the disciples as to which of them would be the greatest. Jesus, knowing their thoughts, took a little child and had him stand beside him. Then he said to them, "Whoever welcomes this little child in my name welcomes me; and whoever welcomes me welcomes the one who sent me. For it is the one who is least among you all who is the greatest."* (**Luke 9:46-48 NLT**)

The disciples had a wrong picture of greatness. Perhaps they thought the greatest was the one who performed the biggest miracles or knew the Scriptures best. Jesus offered a different definition.

He brought a child into the circle and said the one who welcomes a child is the greatest. Why? Because, He explained, "it is the one who is least among you all who is the greatest."

In God's eyes, true greatness is not about seeking prestige, power, or a platform. It is about humbly serving others.

Jesus, who is God Himself, came as a baby to a humble family in a small village. As He grew, He never treated His followers like servants to be ordered around. Instead, He led them patiently and looked for ways to meet their needs.

That is why He teaches that the path to greatness in God's kingdom is to do good consistently without seeking attention or praise. Service levels the playing field. It helps us see one another as God sees us—all equal, all made in His image. And it helps us see God—great, powerful, wonderful, and worthy of all praise—as the One we serve when we serve others.

If we want to love like Jesus, we must pursue His version of greatness. Jesus lived an others-focused life that led Him to hospitality, service, forgiveness, generosity, and sharing God's love with everyone He met. We will explore each of these this week.

So, what are you pursuing in life? The world often invites us to chase "greatness" through personal goals that lead to influence, comfort, or recognition. Jesus invites us to a different path—one where greatness means lifting others up.

Pause and reflect (journal it or talk it over with a friend):

- What does "greatness" look like in your own life right now?

- Who is one person you could serve or encourage this week in a simple, humble way?

Prayer

"God, thank You for showing us through Jesus what true greatness looks like. Help me let go of the world's ideas of success and embrace Your way of humble service. Teach me to love others the way Jesus loved—focusing on their needs and pointing them to You. In Jesus' name, amen."

16

MAKE OTHERS FEEL AT HOME

Have you ever walked into a place that was not your house, yet it felt like home? Maybe it happens at church, in a favorite coffee shop, or at a friend's place. Or perhaps it is a certain person—a family member or friend—who makes you feel completely at ease.

We all feel "at home" when we know we can be ourselves without fear of saying or doing the wrong thing. In those spaces, we feel loved and accepted exactly as we are.

Every one of us longs for that sense of belonging. Jesus understood this deeply, and everywhere He went, He made people feel welcomed and at home. He did this by taking time to invite others into His life, by truly listening, by showing genuine empathy, and by giving them permission to be honest. We call this hospitality.

In Luke 8, we see a list of people who traveled with Jesus during His ministry. These were the individuals He welcomed into His circle. They were imperfect people from different walks of life, but Jesus' hospitality turned them into a kind of family.

The Twelve were with him, and also some women who had been cured of evil spirits and diseases: Mary (called Magdalene) from whom seven demons had come out; Joanna the wife of Chuza, the manager of Herod's household; Susanna; and many others. These women were helping to support them out of their own means. (**Luke 8:1-3 NLT**)

These people could not have been more different. The Twelve came from various social classes and backgrounds. They would have had plenty of reasons to disagree or clash. Yet Jesus welcomed each one just as they were, drawing them into His close community.

Then there is Mary Magdalene. Jesus had freed her from severe spiritual oppression. Despite her difficult past, He welcomed her into His inner circle without hesitation.

And consider Joanna. She was married to the manager of King Herod's household. Herod was no friend to Jesus—in fact, he later ordered the execution of Jesus' cousin, John the Baptist. Yet Jesus welcomed Joanna into His ministry and allowed her to support the group from her own resources.

Hospitality has a way of breaking down barriers and creating unexpected friendships. It invites us to be less judgmental and more curious about others. It helps people discover their God-given value and potential. It builds empathy and turns strangers into neighbors, even family.

Pause and reflect (journal it or talk it over with a friend):

- Think about a time when someone made you feel truly seen, cared for, and included.
- How did their hospitality affect you?
- Now consider this: How might you create that same feeling for someone else?
- What small step could you take this week, partnering with God, to show hospitality to one person?

Prayer

"God, thank You for welcoming me just as I am. Help me learn from Jesus how to make others feel at home in my presence. Give me eyes to see people the way You see them, a heart to listen without judgment, and courage to invite others in. Use me to build connections that reflect Your love. In Jesus' name, amen."

17

GIVING

In the months before Jesus began His public ministry, rumors were spreading about the coming Savior. People had all kinds of ideas about what He would be like, so they went to Jesus' cousin, John the Baptist, for answers.

Many asked how they could prepare for the Savior's arrival. John gave them a clear, practical response:

- *He answered, "Anyone who has two shirts should share with the one who has none, and anyone who has food should do the same."* (**Luke 3:11 NLT**)

According to John, generosity opens our hearts to make room for Jesus.

Generosity is simply sharing what you have to help someone else. That definition is straightforward and beautiful. It includes money, but it also covers so much more—your time, your skills, your attention, your resources, your words, even your presence.

So how do you become a generous person? It is not complicated, but it does require intention and courage. Here are three simple questions to guide you.

First, ask yourself, "What do I really need?" God wants us to enjoy the good things He gives us. We do not have to feel guilty about having what we need. But we do not own our possessions—God does. He entrusts them to us and invites us to share. When we honestly assess what we truly need, it frees us to hold the rest with open hands.

Second, ask yourself, "What do I have to share?" Look around your life. Maybe you have extra time, a skill you have developed, money you could bless someone with, or even encouragement someone needs to hear. No gift is too small. If you have something, there is almost always a way to share it meaningfully.

Third, ask yourself, "What does my community need?" The people around you have real needs you can meet. Perhaps your neighbor is grieving and simply needs your listening ear and kind words. Maybe your local food bank could use volunteers or donations. Your church opens its doors to the community because generous people give regularly. When you pay attention to the needs nearby, it sparks creative ways to be generous.

Many followers of Jesus give regularly from what they earn each week to their church. Why? Because the church is doing God's work right where you live. When we give to the church, we help provide more opportunities for eternal impact—feeding the hungry, supporting families, sharing the hope of Jesus, and meeting needs in practical ways.

Jesus lived with open-handed generosity. He invites each of us to follow His example. You already have what it takes to be generous. Start by answering those three questions: What do I need? What do I have to share? What does my community need?

Pause and reflect (journal it or talk it over with a friend):

- What is one thing you have that you could share this week?

- Who in your life or community might need something you can give—time, a listening ear, a small gift, or encouragement?

Prayer

"God, thank You for everything You have entrusted to me. Help me see my resources with open hands. Show me what I truly need, what I can share, and who around me needs Your love through me. Make me generous like Jesus. In His name, amen."

18

HELPING OTHERS

Today let us talk about a skill Jesus shows us all through the Bible that is easy to miss. On the surface it looks ordinary, but it is actually one of the most powerful ways we can love like Jesus loved.

Jesus was brilliant at noticing needs. Dozens of stories begin with Jesus walking along and suddenly seeing someone who needed help. Sometimes the need was obvious and physical. Other times it was hidden, emotional, or spiritual. Either way, Jesus saw it.

Once He noticed, He used whatever He had to meet the need. Sometimes that meant speaking words of truth or comfort. Sometimes it meant asking the Father for healing and letting the power of the Holy Spirit flow through Him.

As followers of Jesus, we are called to live others-focused lives. One of the clearest ways to do that is by serving. We serve when we notice a need and then use what we have to meet it. Like we talked about yesterday, that often means giving our time, our skills, our resources, or simply our caring presence.

Sometimes the need is bigger than what we can handle on our own. That is not a problem. That is an invitation to ask God for help and watch Him work through us.

Remember, as a follower of Jesus you have the Holy Spirit living inside you.

On the night before He went to the cross, Jesus gathered His disciples for a final meal. In that culture, washing feet was a dirty job usually done by the lowest servant. Yet Jesus, God in human form, got down on His knees and washed the dusty, tired feet of His very imperfect followers.

Afterward He said this:

- *"I have given you an example to follow. Do as I have done to you. I tell you the truth, slaves are not greater than their master. Nor is the messenger more important than the one who sends the message. Now that you know these things, God will bless you for doing them."* (**John 13:15-17 NLT**)

Followers of Jesus look for ways to serve. We keep our eyes open for needs, and with God's help we step in to meet them.

So today, keep your heart and your eyes open. Who around you might need an encouraging word, a listening ear, prayer for healing, or practical help with a task? When you live this others-focused way, you will find yourself growing closer to God than ever.

Pause and reflect (journal it or talk it over with a friend):

- Who is one person you noticed this week who might have a need?
- What is one small way you could serve or encourage them today?

Prayer
"God, thank You for noticing every need in my life. Open my eyes to see the people around me the way You see them. Give me a willing heart and creative ideas to serve them with whatever I have. Let my small acts of love point

others to Jesus. In His name, amen."

19

FORGIVE & FORGIVE SOME MORE

Forgiveness matters deeply to God. He delights in forgiving. Throughout the Bible, we see Him offering forgiveness and fresh starts to all kinds of people, over and over again.

As followers of Jesus, we know exactly what it feels like to be forgiven. We have all made mistakes and hurt others with our choices. Yet God offers us complete forgiveness through Jesus—not because we earned it, but because He loves to forgive.

It is no surprise that Jesus forgave so freely during His time on earth. The Gospels are full of stories where He forgave people's sins. Even at the end of His ministry, when He was beaten, mocked, and crucified, some of His final words were these:

- *Jesus said, "Father, forgive them, for they don't know what they are doing."* (**Luke 23:34 NLT**)

That is how deeply Jesus loves to forgive. He looks past the pain and sees the God-given potential in every person. He does not rush to judgment.

What does this mean for us? If you have followed along, you have probably already guessed: Followers of Jesus forgive others.

One of Jesus' disciples, Peter, once asked Him a very relatable question about forgiveness. He wanted to know how many times he should forgive someone who kept wronging him. Here is what Jesus said:

- *Then Peter came to him and asked, "Lord, how often should I forgive someone who sins against me? Seven times?" "No, not seven times," Jesus replied, "but seventy times seven!"* (**Matthew 18:21-22 NLT**)

Jesus was not telling us to literally count to 490 and then stop. He was saying forgiveness should not have a limit. We keep choosing to forgive, no matter how many times it is needed.

Forgiveness does not mean pretending nothing happened, forgetting the hurt, or excusing bad behavior. It means releasing the desire for revenge or payback. It is a decision to not let anger, bitterness, or pain control your heart and your actions.

Forgiveness can also include healthy boundaries. Sometimes loving someone well means forgiving them while keeping distance to protect your heart and theirs.

We are forgiven people, so we forgive others. It is not always easy. At times it may feel impossible. But forgiving is one of the clearest ways we reflect our forgiving God.

Pause and reflect (journal it or talk it over with a friend):

- Is there someone you are finding it hard to forgive right now?
- What might it look like for you to take one small step toward letting go of

that hurt this week?

Prayer

"Dear God, thank You for forgiving me even when I did not deserve it. Show me anyone I need to forgive, and give me the strength and grace to do it. Help me release bitterness and choose love, just as You have done for me. In Jesus' name, amen."

20

SHARING MY FAITH WITH OTHERS

On the very last day of His ministry on earth, Jesus gave His disciples some final, powerful words:

- *Jesus came and told his disciples, "I have been given all authority in heaven and on earth. Therefore, go and make disciples of all the nations, baptizing them in the name of the Father and the Son and the Holy Spirit. Teach these new disciples to obey all the commands I have given you. And be sure of this: I am with you always, even to the end of the age."* (**Matthew 28:18-20 NLT**)

Let us walk through this passage together...

"All authority in heaven and on earth has been given to me." Jesus is the rightful ruler of everything. He is the King, and we live in His Kingdom. This Kingdom is not like any nation on earth. It is made up of people who choose to live and love the way Jesus does—through humble service, open-handed generosity, warm hospitality, and heartfelt forgiveness.

"Therefore, go and make disciples of all the nations, baptizing them in the name of the Father and the Son and the Holy Spirit. Teach these new disciples to obey all the commands I have given you." Not everyone has yet experienced Jesus' grace, forgiveness, and acceptance. Jesus wants to change that, and He invites us to join Him in the work. He sends us into our neighborhoods, workplaces, schools, and even to the ends of the earth to love people the way He loves them and to show them the joy, purpose, and freedom of a life fully devoted to Him.

This can look like inviting a neighbor to church, sharing your own story of what God has done in your life, offering kindness to a coworker, or simply being present for someone who needs it. There are countless ways God can use you to share and show His love to the people around you.

"And be sure of this: I am with you always, even to the end of the age." When we step out to tell others about Jesus, we are never alone. Jesus promises to be right there with us through the Holy Spirit every step of the way. The Spirit gives us courage, words, and strength as we live out this mission.

How do we obey Jesus' command to share His message and way of life? Followers of Jesus often call this "missions." We get involved locally by getting to know our neighbors, listening to their stories, and looking for practical ways to meet needs in our community. As relationships grow, we naturally share what Jesus is doing in our own lives.

At the same time, we can support global missions. There are full-time missionaries and organizations serving all over the world, focusing on things like Bible translation, education, disaster relief, clean water, and fighting human trafficking. We can support them through prayer, giving financially, or even volunteering when opportunities arise.

Pause and reflect (journal it or talk it over with a friend):

- Who is one person in your life who might not yet know the hope and love Jesus offers?
- What is one small, natural way you could share something about Jesus with them this week?

Prayer

"Jesus, thank You for giving me Your authority and for promising to be with me always. Help me see the people around me with Your eyes. Give me courage and simple opportunities to share Your love and Your story. Use my life to make disciples, right where I am. In Your name, amen."

21

YOU'RE JUST GETTING STARTED

You are almost finished with this book, but your story with Jesus is just getting started.

We are so proud of you for walking through this journey. You showed up, you reflected, you prayed, and you took real steps forward in faith. That matters.

Here are words from one of the earliest followers of Jesus, a man named Paul, written to encourage a group of believers two thousand years ago:

- And I am certain that God, who began the good work within you, will continue his work until it is finally finished on the day when Christ Jesus returns. **(Philippians 1:6 NLT)**

Paul wrote this to people who were doing their best to follow Jesus day by day. They were not perfect. They stumbled sometimes, just like we do. But they were making progress, and Paul was confident God would keep working in them until the very end.

We do not know where you were when Jesus found you or when you first said yes to following Him. We do not know all the challenges you have faced in these past weeks. But we are confident of this: God has started a good work in you, and He will faithfully continue it for the rest of your life.

Paul's prayer for those early believers in the city of Philippi is our prayer for you today:

- *I pray that your love will overflow more and more, and that you will keep on growing in knowledge and understanding.* (**Philippians 1:9 NLT**)

You said yes to Jesus. Now keep saying yes every day!

Seek progress, not perfection. God is love, so He will never abandon you when life gets hard or when you make a mistake. The road will not always feel easy, but as you keep moving forward, you will see God working in and through you as you live and love more like Jesus.

So what happens next?

Your journey of following Jesus is unique to you. You might decide to join a small group and build deeper friendships with other believers. You might choose to get more connected at your church and discover ways to serve. You might look for opportunities to use your gifts to make a difference in your community. Or you might sense God leading you in a completely different direction!

This weekend at church, let us know that you have completed this book. We would love to celebrate with you and help you find your best next step as you continue following Jesus.

Until then, turn the page for a few more ideas and opportunities to keep growing in your faith.

Pause and reflect (journal it or talk it over with a friend):

- What is one thing you have learned or experienced in these weeks that you want to carry forward?
- What is one small next step you feel ready to take as you follow Jesus?

Prayer

"God, thank You for starting this good work in me. Thank You for Your promise to keep going until it is complete. Help me say yes to You every day. Give me courage for the next steps, and fill my heart with overflowing love for You and for others. I trust You with my journey. In Jesus' name, amen."

22

SO, WHAT NOW?

Congratulations—you finished the book! We are genuinely proud of you for walking through this journey. We hope these pages brought you some clarity, a deeper sense of confidence, and real direction as you follow Jesus.

So, what now?

The most important thing is to keep taking the small, daily steps you have been exploring here. There is no single "perfect" path for following Jesus—everyone's story looks a little different—but we have seen some common next steps that help many people grow stronger in their faith.

Take a moment to read through these ideas. Then talk with a pastor, mentor, or trusted friend about what feels like the right next step for you:

- Getting baptized
- Finding a mentor to walk with you
- Joining a team for deeper connection and encouragement
- Sharing your decision to follow Jesus with a friend or family member
- Starting to serve in some way at church or in your community
- Seeking counseling or support if life feels heavy right now

- Inviting someone to church with you
- Giving back to your church and community through time, talents & treasure
- Or whatever other step God's Spirit is quietly nudging you toward

There is no rush or pressure—just honest, open-hearted steps forward.

Once again, congratulations! This book is yours to keep, reread, or pass along to someone who might find it helpful on their own journey.

Pause and reflect (journal it or talk it over with a friend):

- What is one next step that excites you or feels important right now?
- Who could you talk to this week about what comes next for you?

Prayer
"God, thank You for bringing me this far. Thank You for the clarity, the growth, and the hope You have given me. Show me my next step, and give me courage to take it. Keep leading me closer to Jesus every day. In His name, amen."

NEXT STEPS

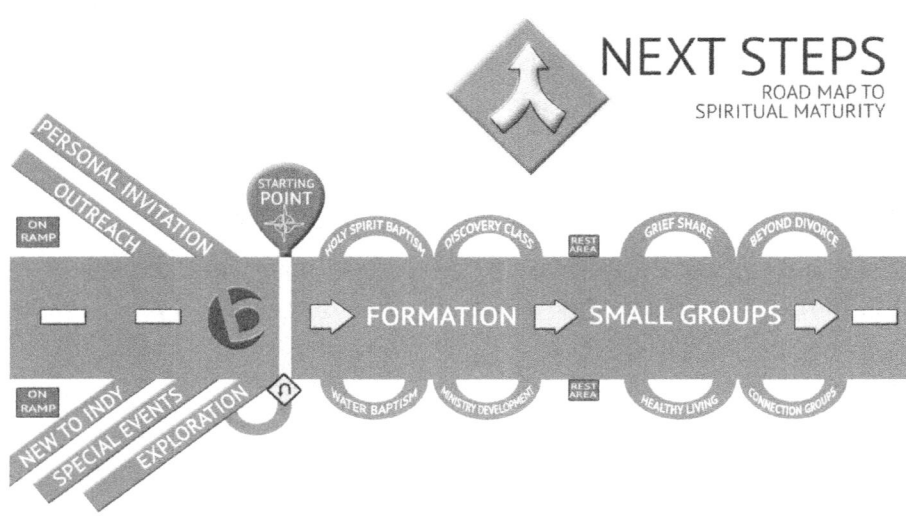

https://www.bfwc.net/next-steps

Following Jesus is the most important decision we will ever make. While believing in Jesus secures our salvation, we are also invited to experience new life here on earth. No one is perfect, but every day, we have the opportunity to grow our faith and our relationship with God.

WHAT IS STARTING POINT?
Starting Point is an exploration of God's grand story, the BFWC story, and where you fit into the narrative. The class is designed to be a conversational environment where you discover more about BFWC and our mission as a church. During our time together, you'll meet our staff, make new friends, and learn how to get involved. Starting Point will help you discover your next step at BFWC.

If you're interested in getting involved at BFWC, Starting Point is for you. Every session includes participants from a wide variety of backgrounds and life stages. Whether you're exploring the faith or a seasoned Christian, we'd love to join you on your spiritual journey.

WATER BAPTISM CLASS
Baptism is an important step of obedience that shows others we have personally trusted Jesus for our salvation. Jesus was baptized when He was on the earth, and we do this to follow His example. When Christians are baptized, they are submerged under water to identify with the death and burial of Jesus and raised out of the water to identify with His resurrection. We believe that water baptism is a public declaration of three important things: you are a follower of Jesus Christ, you are beginning a changed life in Christ, and you are part of a new family.

EXPLORATION CLASS
Following Jesus is a big decision and there's a lot you may not yet understand about the intricacies of your faith. We invite you to join the Exploration Class

to answer any questions you have as you grow in your faith. In the meantime, begin reading your Bible. You can start with the book of John.

DISCOVERY CLASS

Dive into the details of your personality, discover your gifts, and see how your design reveals your purpose in life and your best fit in ministry.

UNDERSTANDING THE BAPTISM IN THE HOLY SPIRIT CLASS

In this class, we will lay the foundation of Scripture for you to realize why you are eligible to receive this gift!

MINISTRY 101 CLASS

We believe God has a plan for your life & we're ready to equip you for that plan! In this class, you'll be challenged, prepared & encouraged to fulfill your life call while learning the ropes of ministry & how to function in health at BFWC.

NOTES

NOTES

NOTES

NOTES

QUICK OVERVIEW

1.Joining the Local Church

God places great value on being part of a local church. The Bible says:

- *And let us not neglect our meeting together, as some people do, but encourage one another, especially now that the day of his return is drawing near.* **(Hebrews 10:25 NLT)**

Church members have a responsibility to encourage and pray for one another. There are special blessings that come when you connect with a local church. You come under the prayer covering of your pastor, and healing and restoration become available because God places healing in the storehouse of the local church.

We draw strength from one another in our walk with God. Imagine one burning coal placed alone in a pit—it soon cools and goes out. But when added to a group of hot coals, it stays burning and adds heat to the others. Our faith grows stronger when we pray and believe together.

- *Two people are better off than one, for they can help each other succeed. If one person falls, the other can reach out and help. But someone who falls alone is in real trouble.* (**Ecclesiastes 4:9-10 NLT**)

The enemy knows that if you isolate yourself from other believers, it becomes easier to bring confusion, discouragement, or temptation into your life.

One of the most important reasons to join a local church is that God has assigned each of us a specific place in the Body of Christ.

- *God has appointed in the church first apostles, second prophets, third teachers, then miracles, then gifts of healing, helping, administrating, and various kinds of tongues.* (**1 Corinthians 12:28 NLT, adapted**)

God has something unique for you to do in His Body. No one else can fill your place. That is why it is vital to come under the authority of your pastor and begin fulfilling the plan God has for your life.

If you have not yet found a church home, we would love for you to join us for our Sunday Worship Experiences (8:45 & 11 AM) and Wednesday MDWK (7:00 PM). Connect with our Starting Point Class.

2.Water Baptism

Now that you have asked Jesus into your heart as Lord and Savior, you may be wondering, "What do I do next?"

- *Therefore go and make disciples of all nations, baptizing them in the name of the Father and of the Son and of the Holy Spirit.* (**Matthew 28:19 NLT**)

The Bible teaches that all believers should be baptized in water. Baptism is not a ritual; it is an outward declaration to the world that Jesus Christ is Lord of your life.

When you go under the water in baptism, you identify with Christ's death on the cross and burial in the tomb. When you come up out of the water, you identify with His resurrection to new life. Your old sinful nature is buried with Christ, and you rise with a new nature in Him.

3. Now You Need the Power of the Holy Spirit

Before the day of Pentecost, the disciples were afraid of persecution and threats. But when the Holy Spirit came upon them, ordinary fishermen became bold world-changers. After receiving the baptism of the Holy Spirit, they feared nothing. Prison could not stop them, torture could not silence them, and persecution only made them stronger.

If you need breakthrough in your life, you need the power of the Holy Spirit and a fresh baptism of boldness. The Holy Spirit gives you strength beyond what you have in your own power.

If you desire this power, all you have to do is ask.

- *And so I tell you, keep on asking, and you will receive what you ask for. Keep on seeking, and you will find. Keep on knocking, and the door will be opened to you.* (**Luke 11:9 NLT**)

The Bible describes what happened on the day of Pentecost:

- *Suddenly, there was a sound from heaven like the roaring of a mighty windstorm, and it filled the house where they were sitting. Then, what looked like flames or tongues of fire appeared and settled on each of them. And everyone present was filled with the Holy Spirit and began speaking in other languages, as the Holy Spirit gave them this ability.* (**Acts 2:2-4 NLT**)

God is no respecter of persons. What He did for the disciples, He will do for you. The infilling of the Holy Spirit is a free gift, just like salvation. If you want this power in your life, follow these simple steps:

Step 1: Praise Him.
Start by thanking the Lord for His goodness, grace, and mercy in your life.

Step 2: Pray this prayer:
Heavenly Father, thank You that I am born again and on my way to heaven. Today I desire to be filled with the power of the Holy Spirit. Your Word says, "For everyone who asks receives…" I ask You to fill me with the Spirit to overflowing.

Step 3: Close your eyes and raise your hands to the Lord.
This is a simple sign of surrender to Him.

Step 4: Open your mouth and speak out by faith.
Say nothing in English. Your heavenly language will rise up inside you and flow out. Make the sounds—the Holy Spirit will form the words. Do not worry about what it sounds like or who might hear. Lock in with God. Give Him your tongue and your breath. Just open your mouth and begin to speak. Let it flow.

If you prayed to receive the Holy Spirit and did not experience it right away, do not be discouraged. There is nothing wrong with you. Sometimes people need a little help. Feel free to come to the altar at the end of any service and ask a minister to pray with you.

QUICK OVERVIEW

4. If You Need Healing

It is never God's will for you or your family to suffer with sickness or disease. His Word says:

- *Dear friend, I hope all is well with you and that you are as healthy in body as you are strong in spirit.* (**3 John 1:2 NLT**)

Healing is for today, and it is for you! The enemy wants you to believe God sends sickness to punish you, but that is a lie. The Bible says:

- *He personally carried our sins in his body on the cross so that we can be dead to sin and live for what is right. By his wounds you are healed.* (**1 Peter 2:24 NLT**)

When Jesus died, He made provision for healing. When sickness comes, recognize it is not from God and begin speaking His Word over your situation.

Here are some powerful Scriptures on healing:

- *My child, pay attention to what I say; listen carefully to my words. Don't lose sight of them. Let them penetrate deep into your heart, for they bring life to those who find them, and healing to their whole body.* (**Proverbs 4:20-22 NLT**)

- *I tell you, you can pray for anything, and if you believe that you've received it, it will be yours.* (**Mark 11:24 NLT**)

- *Are any of you sick? You should call for the elders of the church to come and pray over you, anointing you with oil in the name of the Lord.* (**James 5:14 NLT**)

- *Let all that I am praise the Lord; may I never forget the good things he does for me. He forgives all my sins and heals all my diseases.* (**Psalm 103:2-3 NLT**)

Do not get discouraged!

If healing does not appear immediately after you pray, do not lose heart. Healing is already yours. Continue speaking God's Word over your body. Trust in the Lord with all your heart and lean not on your own understanding (Proverbs 3:5). God's Word will not return empty—it will accomplish what He desires (Isaiah 55:11). Your healing will manifest because Scripture declares: *"By His wounds you are healed!"* (**1 Peter 2:24**).

5. Priorities for a Successful Start as a New Believer

1. Find a good Bible-believing church and become an active part of it. Experience the power of God flowing freely. *"Let us not neglect meeting together."* If you have not found a church home yet, we would love to have you join us for our Sunday Worship Experiences (8:45 & 11 AM) and Wednesday MDWK (7:00 p.m.) services while you search.

2. Be baptized in water as Jesus commanded all new believers. (Matthew 28:19; Mark 16:16; Acts 2:38)

3. Read your Bible every day to grow, receive direction, and be strengthened in your spirit. As you read, God speaks to you. (2 Timothy 2:15; Psalm 119:11; Matthew 4:4)

4. Pray every day. Prayer is simply talking to God. Set aside time in a quiet place to be alone with Him. Consistency is key. (Luke 11:1; James 5:16; Philippians 4:6-8)

5. Begin tithing as God commands. "Tithe" means tenth—one tenth of your income belongs to God. He entrusts us with 90% but asks for the first 10%. (Numbers 18:24-28; Malachi 3:8-10)

6. Get involved in the ministries of your church. This allows you to use your God-given gifts and talents. (Ecclesiastes 9:10; 1 Corinthians 12)

7. Avoid old habits, places, or people that could cause you to stumble. You have a new life in Christ. Enjoy the freedom God has given you by developing a new lifestyle. (Romans 8:1-2; 2 Corinthians 6:14-18; 1 Thessalonians 5:22)

We believe that as you put these things into practice in your daily walk, you will grow strong in your knowledge of our Lord and Savior Jesus Christ. If you walk with God, He will walk with you.

We rejoice that you have accepted Christ as your Savior today. Our prayer is that you continue to grow in God's grace, which is able to keep you from falling.

We are here for you—reach out anytime. Welcome to the family!

Contact info@bfwc.net

Made in the USA
Coppell, TX
01 February 2026

70249862R00056